Tea & Cake

with the Saints

A Catholic Young Lady's Introduction
to Hospitality and the Home Arts

by Alice M. Cantrell

Little Way Press

Twain Harte, California

About the Author

Alice Cantrell lives in South Louisiana where she and her husband home-school their five children and strive to live a simple, hospitable life.

Also by Alice Cantrell

Sewing with Saint Anne: A Sewing Book for Catholic Girls

Acknowledgments

I would like to thank my patient, loving and supportive husband and children for putting up with the writing of yet another little book. Especially for pitching in and helping out around the house in so many ways.

A special thanks also to Saints Martha and Mary, who have taught me much about the virtue of hospitality, and intercede for me daily.

Back cover photo credit: Anna Cantrell, Hollis Yarborough, and Amelie Desormeaux

Book design by RoseMary C. Johnson

ISBN: 978-0-9764691-5-5

Little Way Press
Twain Harte, California
www.littlewaypress.com

Distributed by Catholic Heritage Curricula
P.O. Box 125, Twain Harte, CA 95383
1-800-490-7713 www.chcweb.com

Contents

Throughout the book you will find new terms which may not be familiar to you. Many of these words will be in *italics*. The definition of these words can be found in the Glossary beginning on page 107.

Note to Parents

The purpose of this book is to introduce a few of the basic homemaking arts to our young ladies, while helping them to foster a love of service to others by practicing the biblical virtue of hospitality—all from a Catholic perspective. (It is not however, intended to be an all-inclusive home economics text.) There are dozens and dozens of different possibilities for celebrating saints' feast days or special Holy days and *name days*. For the purposes of this work we only present a few suggestions for each season, but the ideas and recipes included in this little book will work for any special day.

Most of the recipes included here are quite simple, but for the younger child, parental assistance will be necessary. Please use your judgment, and knowledge of your daughter's experience in the kitchen, to guide you in allowing her the use of the stove, oven and sharp knives.

Some basic sewing skills are needed for a few of the ideas in this book. Any beginner level sewing book should provide the instruction required. If you would like a beginning sewing book with a Catholic perspective, *Sewing with Saint Anne* (available from Catholic Heritage Curricula) contains detailed instructions for almost all the projects mentioned in this book.

Above all, let your love for one another be constant, for love covers a multitude of sins. Be mutually hospitable without complaining. As generous distributors of God's manifold grace, put your gifts at the service of one another, each in the measure he has received.

—1 PETER 4:8-10

Introduction

The dictionary describes hospitality as "cordial reception: kindness in welcoming guests or strangers." The Bible mentions it many times in the Old Testament as well as the New. (Genesis 18:1–8, 2 Kings 4:1–7 , Matthew 10:40, Romans 12:13, Hebrews 13:2, and 1 Peter 4:8–10 are just a very few.) Throughout the Scriptures we see one example after another of God's people offering what little they have in hospitality. Indeed, Jesus calls us all to hospitality when he says, "I assure you, as often as you did it for one of my least brothers, you did it for me." (Matthew 25:40)

Hospitality does not have to be elaborate or difficult. It can begin right at home with your siblings and parents. It can be as simple as a picnic with a friend to celebrate their name day (or feast day) or surprising your sister with breakfast in bed. Many of the ideas in this book will focus on using various saints' feast days as the occasion for practicing hospitality in the form of simple tea parties, but as you will see, almost all of the ideas given can be used for any occasion you can dream up! Actual tea does not even have to be present if you and your guest do not care for it. Lemonade or hot chocolate will work just as well.

Tea was first introduced to Great Britain in the mid-1600's. By 1700 it was a regular part of English life and was quickly replacing coffee as the beverage of choice. The tradition of "afternoon tea" is attributed to a

British Duchess named Anna. (She was the seventh Duchess of Bedford and lived from 1783 to 1857.) In those days, it was the custom in England to eat a large breakfast and then a late dinner. Becoming quite hungry during this long stretch of time between meals, Anna began to order tea, cakes and biscuits to be brought to her room at about four in the afternoon. Other upper class women heard of the Duchess's afternoon teas, and the custom began to spread until it became so popular that soon everyone was enjoying their "tea time."

Before You Begin

There are a few simple things to remember before trying out any of the recipes in this book:

- Make sure your hands and nails are clean. If you have long hair, it is a good idea to tie it back. A scarf is handy to have and can keep back any length hair. (See the next page for instructions for a simple scarf.)

- Put on your apron to protect your clothes.

- Read through the entire recipe before beginning.

- Gather all the tools and ingredients you will need before beginning. (Don't forget the potholders for removing hot pans from the oven!)

- If you have very little experience in the kitchen, you may want to ask a parent for help.

- **Be safe! When using sharp knives or vegetable peelers, always cut away from your hand, and make sure to keep pot handles on the stove top turned in so that they do not accidentally get bumped into. Always use pot holders when removing pans from the oven.**

A Simple Scarf

Using a scrap of light- to medium-weight fabric, cut into a 20-inch square, finish the raw edges either by turning and stitching or with a simple zigzag stitch. Next, fold as shown in the illustration.

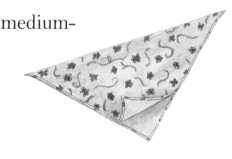

Also, a pretty cloth napkin made from a lightweight fabric will work just as well, and you will not have to finish the raw edges. Just make sure that it is about a 20-inch square.

Measuring Ingredients

When measuring the ingredients for a recipe, especially when baking, it is important to measure correctly. For measuring dry ingredients (flour, sugar, spices, etc.), in both measuring cups and spoons, the method is the same. Carefully scoop your cup or spoon into the dry ingredient. Do not pack the ingredient into the cup or spoon as you will end up using too much for the recipe. Your dry ingredient will be mounded up above the rim of your measuring tool. While holding the cup or spoon over the container of the dry ingredient, use the back of a table knife to scrape across the top, creating a level surface.

When using a liquid measuring cup for wet ingredients (water, milk, etc.), fill the clear glass (or plastic) measuring cup with the amount of liquid the recipe calls for, and then set it on the counter or table and stoop down so that the cup is at eye level. When looking at it from the side like this, you can see clearly if the liquid comes to the appropriate mark.

Kitchen Cleanup

It is very important to leave the kitchen clean and in order. A great way to make after-cooking cleanup easier is to fill the sink about half-way with hot, soapy water before beginning a recipe. This way, you can drop in dirty utensils, bowls, etc. as you finish with them. By soaking them in the soapy water, instead of letting the food dry on them, they will be much easier to clean.

A great all-purpose cleaner that you probably have right in the kitchen is white vinegar. By keeping a small spray bottle filled with plain vinegar handy, you will have a frugal and safe cleaner to clean counter tops, stovetop and table. (Make sure that your spray bottle is clearly labeled "Vinegar.") Studies have shown that a straight 5% solution (diluted with water to 5% acidity) of white vinegar, such as you can get at the grocery store, kills 99% of bacteria, 82% of mold and 80% of germs and viruses.

When you are finished cooking, and you have washed the dishes, make sure to wipe down all surfaces (counter tops, stove top and table) with either soap and water (using a small dish cloth and some fresh soapy water in the sink) or vinegar (spray on, then wipe off with a small dish cloth.) Make sure to check the cabinet doors below the area where you were working for any food drips that may need wiping up. If there is food stuck hard to the top of the stove, simply leave a little water or vinegar on it while you clean the other areas of the kitchen. When you come back to it, it will have softened and will wipe off easily. Lastly, wipe up any drips or spills on the kitchen floor, and sweep up any crumbs you may have dropped.

Equivalent Measures Chart

Below is an equivalent measures chart. This will be useful if you are trying to halve, double or even triple a recipe. (Keep in mind that in some recipe books "tablespoon" will be abbreviated "tbsp" and "teaspoon" will be "tsp.")

Equivalent Measures

3 teaspoons = 1 tablespoon

4 tablespoons = ¼ cup

5 ⅓ tablespoons = ⅓ cup

8 tablespoons = ½ cup

16 tablespoons = 1 cup

1 tablespoon = ½ fluid ounce

1 cup = 8 fluid ounces

1 cup = ½ pint

2 cup = 1 pint

4 cups = 1 quart

2 pints = 1 quart

4 quarts = 1 gallon

A Notebook

I n the not so distant past, it was quite common for the lady of the house to keep a household record book. It was sort of like a journal of all her home-keeping chores, activities, recipes, etc. (Usually a separate book held the household accounts wherein a careful record of all the family's expenses was kept.) These valuable books were passed down from generation to generation filled with the wisdom and experiences of grandmothers and great grandmothers.

A young lady of today might consider starting such a notebook or journal herself. The notebook suggested here could be as simple or as elaborate as you would like and would be filled gradually over many months or even years. It could be made from a three-ring binder or even a scrapbook. A few things that could be included in your notebook are your favorite recipes, decorating ideas, organizing and cleaning info, photos of a completed sewing project or cake, hospitality ideas and more!

If you are using a binder, a standard sized one (that is, ½ to ¾ inch thick) will probably be the easiest to use and to find dividers and page protectors to fit. The dividers make it easy to find the various sections in your notebook quickly, and the page protectors are nice for keeping photos, clippings, recipe cards, pressed flowers and other pasted-in things safe from smudges and splatters. Many scrapbooks already come  with clear, plastic sleeves for protecting the contents of their pages.

Decorate your homemaking notebook and make it beautiful so that it will be a pleasure to use. If you are going to use a binder, the type with the clear pocket on the cover will allow you to design a lovely cover and slip it right it. Magazine clippings of flowers, stickers or even your own artwork can be used on the cover. Also, the scrapbooking supplies at your local craft store can provide you with much inspiration for decorating your notebook.

If you are using dividers (the ones with pockets are especially nice) for your notebook, below is a list of some suggested topics:

- Recipes—these could be written-in or pasted-in recipe cards and clippings.

- Home keeping—cleaning information and tips, organizing ideas and decorating hints

- Gardening—garden notes (what grew well, what did not) photos and plans

- Hospitality—ideas for ways and occasions to practice hospitality, photos of tea parties

- Gift Ideas—a list of easy and frugal things to make for gifts

- Projects—this could be a list of current or future sewing or crafting projects.

- Personal Accounts—a place to keep track of the money you earn, spend and your personal savings goals

- Notes—sometimes it's nice to have a section with simple lined paper for jotting down your thoughts and ideas.

Your homemaking notebook will not fill up overnight. It will be a gradual process, but one that will be very enjoyable. Once you start looking for things to include in your notebook, you will soon begin see ideas everywhere!

Brewing Tea

Brewing tea is quite simple and will become even easier after you have done it a few times. Follow the steps below for a perfect pot of tea. Don't forget to read through all the directions before beginning!

1. Fill your tea kettle with fresh water and set it on the stove to heat. (A tea kettle is used on the stove to heat water while a teapot is used to steep and serve the tea.)

2. While waiting for the water to boil, run hot tap water into your teapot to warm it and choose the type of tea you will brew. If you are using loose tea (tea that has not been packaged into tea bags), place one spoonful for each cup of tea into the warmed pot. If you are using tea bags, use one bag per cup of tea. (The teapot is not needed if you are using tea bags, as they can be placed directly into the cup, and the hot water poured over them.)

3. When the water has come to a boil, turn off the stove and pour the appropriate amount of water into the teapot. To determine the correct amount of water, you must first know your teapot size. For example, if you have a 6-cup pot and you want to make three cups of tea, you will need to fill the warmed teapot about halfway up.

4. Place the cover on the teapot and let the tea steep three to five minutes or according to the directions on the package of tea. Herbal teas will require a slightly longer steeping time than black teas, and green teas need less time than black. (If all this talk of green, black and herbal teas is new to you, see the box below.)

5. When the steeping time is up, open the teapot lid and stir the brew slightly. Replace the lid and you are ready to pour! If you are using loose tea, you will need to place a tea strainer over each cup to catch the leaves as you pour. Milk, sugar, lemon and honey all go very well with hot tea. Do not combine milk and lemon in the same cup, however; the acid in the lemon juice will cause the milk to curdle.

Basic Tea Types

All tea is from the leaves of the evergreen shrub called *camellia sinensis*. The three basic tea types are *black tea, green tea* and *oolong tea*. Black is made from leaves that have been fully oxidized or fermented. The flavor is stronger, and the color darker. Green tea is withered and then immediately steamed or heated to prevent oxidation. It has a delicate taste and light green color. To make oolong tea, the leaves are partly *oxidized* (exposed to air), making it a combination of both black and green. Flavored teas are simply any of the above teas with added fruit, spices or other flavorings. Herbal "teas" are not technically tea, but are actually *tisanes* or infusions. They can be a single ingredient or a blend of herbs, spices, flowers or fruits.

Tea Cup History

Tea first arrived in Europe from China in 1610. With the introduction of this new beverage came the tea sets in which the Chinese drank their tea. The Chinese people used small bowls with saucers made from a very fine pottery, unlike anything the Europeans had ever seen before. The Europeans soon called this beautiful form of pottery "China."

The small, handle-less tea bowls were called "cans" by the British and it was considered quite acceptable and polite to pour one's hot tea into the saucer to cool and then sip it from the dish. This is where the term "dish of tea" comes from.

Phebe was making tea by the study fire, for the Doctor had forgotten to eat and drink since Rose was ill, and Aunt Plenty insisted on his having a "good cordial dish of tea" after his exertions.

—EIGHT COUSINS, *LOUISA MAY ALCOTT*

In the mid-1700's, handles were added to the small bowls, and they began to look more like the teacups of today.

"It is sad to see a great girl wasting these precious hours so. Now, my boys have studied all day, and Mac is still at his books, I've no doubt, while you have not had a lesson since you came, I suspect."

"I've had five to-day, ma'am," was Rose's very unexpected answer… "…I have collected some useful information about China, which you may like, especially the teas. The best are Lapsing Souchong, Assam Pekoe, rare Ankoe, Flowery Pekoe, Howqua's mixture, Scented Caper, Padral tea, black Congou, and green Twankey. Shanghai is on the Woosung River. Hong Kong means 'Island of Sweet waters.' Singapore is 'Lion's Town.' 'Chops' are the boats they live in; and they drink tea out of little saucers. Principal productions are porcelain, tea, cinnamon, shawls, tin, tamarinds and opium. They have beautiful temples and queer gods; and in Canton is the Dwelling of the Holy Pigs, fourteen of them, very big, and all blind."

—Eight Cousins, Louisa May Alcott

Tea & Cake

Winter

The Snowflake

Before I melt,
Come, look at me!
This lovely icy filigree!
Of a great forest
In one night
I make a wilderness
Of white:
By skyey cold
Of crystals made,
All softly, on
Your finger laid,
I pause, that you
My beauty see:
Breathe; and I vanish
Instantly.

—WALTER DE LA MARE

The night was clear and frosty, all ebony of shadow and silver of snowy slope; big stars were shining over the silent fields; here and there the dark pointed firs stood up with snow powdering their branches and the wind whistling through them. Anne thought it was truly delightful to go skimming through all this mystery and loveliness with your bosom friend who had been so long estranged.

—ANNE OF GREEN GABLES, *L.M. MONTGOMERY*

Brrrr! As the cold winds begin to blow and the snowflakes swirl, it is a wonderful time to invite a friend (or even a sibling or parent!) for a cozy cup of tea or hot chocolate. During these blustery days, the Church celebrates many beautiful feasts, the greatest of which is the birth of our Lord Jesus!

The chilly months of winter provide many occasions for hospitality. In December, a Christmas-themed tea party would be beautiful, but also consider one on the 13th in honor of St. Lucy. Among other things, she is the patroness of authors and writers. Perhaps take the occasion of her feast day to start a book club with a few friends and name it in her honor. Or maybe in January, after the holiday excitement has past, hold a tea honoring St. Agnes of Rome (who is one of the patronesses of girls!) for one dear friend. And don't forget St. Blaise in February, the patron saint of coughs and throats! Why not take a small gift—a mug with a few tea bags tucked inside—to a friend suffering from a cold?

December, *the month dedicated to the Divine Childhood:*
   St. Nicholas of Myra (6th)
   Our Lady of Guadalupe (12th)
   St. Lucy of Syracuse (13th)
   Christmas (25th)
January, *the month dedicated to the Holy Name of Jesus:*
   Feast of Mary the Mother of God (1st)
   St. Elizabeth Ann Seton (4th)
   St. Agnes of Rome (21st)
February, *the month dedicated to the Passion of Our Lord:*
   St. Blaise (3rd)
   St. Scholastica (10th)
   St. Valentine of Rome (14th)

Below are a few menu suggestions to help warm up your winter tea parties. The recipes listed below are only suggestions and would work well for any of the above feasts.

Menu

Tea or Hot Chocolate

Cheddar Muffins

Spice Cake

Cream Cheese Mints

Hot Chocolate Mix

(Makes 4 servings)

Ingredients:

1⅓   cups powdered milk

⅛   cup cocoa

⅓   cup sugar

   Mini Marshmallows (optional)

Directions:

1. Mix the ingredients together and store in an airtight container in a cool, dry place.

2. When you are ready to use, scoop out ½ cup of the mix and place into an empty 12-ounce mug. Fill the mug the rest of the way up with boiling water, but leave room for a few marshmallows!

3. Add marshmallows or even whipped cream, if you prefer.

Cheddar Muffins
(Makes 1 dozen)

When mixing *quickbreads*, be careful not to over mix.
Stir batter until just blended.

Ingredients:

1¾ cups all-purpose flour

¼ cup sugar

2 teaspoons baking powder

1 teaspoon salt

1 cup milk

¼ cup cooking oil

1 egg

¾ cup shredded cheddar cheese

Directions:

1. Preheat oven to 400°.

2. Mix all of the *dry ingredients* and the grated cheese together with a wire whisk or mixing spoon in a medium-sized mixing bowl.

3. In a separate bowl, combine the *wet ingredients* and mix thoroughly with the whisk or spoon.

4. Now carefully pour the wet ingredients into the bowl containing the dry ingredients and mix just until combined. A few lumps are okay; do not over mix!

5. Carefully spoon batter into a greased muffin tin, or one lined with paper bake cups, and bake for about

20 minutes, or until an inserted toothpick comes out clean with no batter sticking to it.

Baking Soda and Baking Powder

Both baking soda and baking powder are used to make baked goods "rise." Baking soda is pure sodium bicarbonate, and when it comes into contact with moisture and an acidic ingredient, such as honey, buttermilk or chocolate, a chemical reaction takes place. During this reaction, tiny bubbles of carbon dioxide form and expand, as the baked item cooks, causing the muffin, cookie or cake to rise. Baking powder contains baking soda along with a dry acid (usually cream of tartar) and a starch.

Yeast was the primary leavening ingredient used up until the late 18th century. After that time, sodium bicarbonate became gradually more popular. Baking powder did not come into common use until the mid-1800's.

The flower-bed was not quite bare. It was bare of flowers because the perennial plants had been cut down for their winter rest, but there were tall shrubs and low ones which grew together at the back of the bed, and as the robin hopped about under them she saw him hop over a small pile of freshly turned up earth.

—THE SECRET GARDEN, *FRANCES HODGSON BURNETT*

Cream Cheese Mints

(Makes about 45 mints)

Ingredients:

1	3-ounce package cream cheese, *softened*
2¼	cups powdered sugar
¼	teaspoon peppermint flavoring
⅛	cup granulated sugar for rolling mints in

Directions:

1. In a small bowl, combine the *softened* cream cheese, powdered sugar and peppermint flavoring.

2. Blend the ingredients together thoroughly until the mixture resembles dough. You will probably need to use your hands to knead in the last of the powdered sugar. (You can add more powdered sugar if your "dough" is too sticky.)

3. Shape mixture into balls the size of large marbles, and roll in the granulated sugar. Slightly flatten the balls into a circle about the size of a quarter and arrange on pretty little plates or saucers. Store any extras in an airtight container. Enjoy!

A Gift Idea

These little mints also make a lovely gift! Simply line a small box or container with a piece of waxed paper cut into the same shape and size as the box. Gently lay the mints inside and separate two or more layers of the candy with waxed paper. You can also re-use small empty candy tins by gluing your own creative label over the existing one. What a delicious treat to bring as a *hostess gift*!

Spice Cake
(Serves 8)

This simple little cake will make the whole house smell delicious!

Ingredients:

1⅓	cups all-purpose flour
⅔	cup sugar
2	teaspoons baking powder
1	teaspoon cinnamon
¼	teaspoon nutmeg
⅛	teaspoon ground cloves
⅔	cup milk
¼	cup butter or margarine, softened
1	egg
1	teaspoon vanilla

Directions:

1. Preheat oven to 375°.

2. In a large mixing bowl combine flour, sugar, baking powder and spices.

3. Add the milk, softened butter or margarine, egg and vanilla and beat with an electric mixer on low speed until combined, then beat on medium speed for one

minute. You can use a wire whisk if you do not have an electric mixer.

4. Pour the batter into a *greased and floured* (see side box for more information) 8-inch round or square baking pan.

5. Bake for 25 to 30 minutes or until a toothpick inserted in the center of the cake comes out without any raw batter sticking to it.

6. Let the cake cool for 15 minutes in the pan. Then remove from the pan and let cool completely on a wire cooling rack.

7. When the cake is completely cool, set it on a plate and drizzle vanilla icing (see recipe on next page) all over it. Yum!

Greasing & Flouring

Using your hand or a paper towel spread an even layer of cooking oil over the bottom and sides of the cake pan.

Next, sprinkle a little flour in the bottom of the pan. Start with about a teaspoon and add more if necessary.

Tilt and tap the pan until the flour covers all the surfaces. Now tap out any excess flour. Your pan is now ready for the cake batter to be poured in.

Easy Vanilla Icing

Place 2 cups of powdered sugar in a small bowl. Add ½ teaspoon of vanilla and 3 tablespoons of milk. Stir well and drizzle or pour over your cake. If possible, let cake stand two hours before slicing to allow icing to harden.

A Recipe Card

If you would like to share these (or any other) recipes with a friend, simply make copies of the recipe card provided below. Print them onto cardstock or any other stiff paper and cut out with plain or decorative-edged scissors. These make nice additions to your homemaking notebook, and it is also a thoughtful gesture to include the recipe when giving a gift of food.

A Recipe For:

More Ideas

If you are having only one guest, instead of serving your tea at the family dining table, consider using only a small folding table pulled up next to the fireplace. This provides a cozy and fun atmosphere!

If several guests are expected, make beautiful place cards using colored papers and decorative-edged scissors and display them using curtain rings with attached clips. These rings double as elegant napkin rings and also hold a place card! A set of these would be a nice addition to your hope chest, also.

It is fun to make gifts for friends and family. Here is an idea for an easy-to-make gift to give for Christmas or any other occasion.

Medal Marker

A "medal marker" is simply a book marker made using a medal of a favorite saint or perhaps a scapular or miraculous medal. To make one, all you will need is a medal and a 10–12-inch length of grosgrain ribbon. (It can be anywhere from ¾ inch to 1 inch

wide.) There is a product called "Fray Check" (available in the sewing section of craft stores) which is also helpful. Fray Check prevents the edges of the ribbon from becoming frayed with use.

1. Cut the ends of your ribbon as shown below and apply Fray Check to the cut edges. Allow to dry for about 15 minutes.

Step 1: Cut one end straight (left) and one end with a 'V' (right).

2. Next, turn the straight end up ½" and press carefully with a warm iron. Now fold inward to form a point. Tack in place with a few stitches of matching thread.

3. To complete the medal marker, flip the ribbon over and attach the medal with a few stitches of the same matching thread. That's it!

For another delicious and easy winter gift, pour 1 cup of the hot chocolate mix into a zip-top sandwich bag and attach a copy of the tag below with a pretty ribbon. This little gift is especially nice tucked inside a nice ceramic mug. What a great way to warm up a friend or neighbor!

To:

From:

Hot Chocolate Mix

To make a cup of hot chocolate, place 1/2 cup of this mix into an empty 12 oz. mug and fill up the mug with boiling water. Stir till dissolved and add marshmallows or whipped cream. Enjoy!

Stopping by Woods on a Snowy Evening

Whose woods these are I think I know.
His house is in the village though;
He will not see me stopping here
To watch his woods fill up with snow.

My little horse must think it queer
To stop without a farmhouse near
Between the woods and frozen lake
The darkest evening of the year.

He gives his harness bells a shake
To ask if there is some mistake.
The only other sound's the sweep
Of easy wind and downy flake.

The woods are lovely, dark and deep.
But I have promises to keep,
And miles to go before I sleep,
And miles to go before I sleep.

—ROBERT FROST

On Manners

Emily Post was the foremost writer in America on the topic of manners and etiquette for many years. She believed that the basis of all good manners was putting others before ourselves. She said, "Manners are a sensitive awareness of the feelings of others. If you have that awareness, you have good manners, no matter what fork you use."

Good manners are just that simple. Yes, there are various rules to follow when dining at a fancy restaurant and for other occasions, but for most circumstances in your life the simple rule above will suffice. Below are a few guidelines to help make practicing hospitality easier and more pleasant:

* Always dress nicely and neatly.

* Greet guests warmly, with a smile. "I'm so glad you could come!"

* If you are hosting more than one other person, make sure no one is left out of the conversation.

* It helps to specify certain hours for your guests when you invite them. For example, "come for tea from 3 pm–5 pm." Then they are spared the uncomfortable task of trying to decide when the appropriate time to leave is.

* Ask politely for something out of your reach to be passed to you.

- And of course, all those things your mother tells you frequently: place your napkin in your lap, sit up straight, elbows off the table, etc.

Using good manners is not limited to while your guests are with you. For example, it is very good manners to send a "thank you" note to your friends after they have had you over for a visit. These little notes do not have to be fancy and can be made at home very easily using an unlined 4" x 6" index card. A quick trim along the edges with a pair of decorative-edged scissors will make it look extra nice. A simple thank you note might read:

Date

_Dear _____,_

I had such a lovely time at your house yesterday. Thank you so much for having me.

Your friend,

_____

For a larger event or more formal tea party, you might like to send an invitation to your guests. Invitations should be sent one to two weeks before your planned event and should include the following information:

Miss Anna Smith

requests the pleasure

of your company

for a tea party to celebrate

the feast of St. Maria Goretti,

on Friday, the 6th of July,

from 3 pm to 5 pm,

in the Smith's back yard.

Please R. S. V. P. 123-4567

The traditional layout for an invitation is to center the text on the card. (Once again, a blank 4" x 6" index card will work very well.) The exact wording can be whatever you would like: plain and simple, a poem, silly and fun. The important thing is to include all the necessary information for the person receiving the invitation. The letters R.S.V.P. stand for "répondez, s'il vous plait," which is French for "reply, if you please." When you see these letters at the bottom of an invitation (usually followed by a telephone number), it is a request for the recipient to make a quick call to the hostess of the party and let her know whether or not she will be attending.

One final thought: save a copy of the invitations you send out in your homemaking notebook, along with a few notes about the event. This will be helpful information to look back on when you are planning future celebrations.

If you are looking for activities that you can do when hosting several friends at one time, why not try one of the ideas below!

Host a Cookie Exchange!

A cookie exchange is perfect for an Advent season gathering of several of your friends.

The basic idea is very simple: each guest (and you!) bakes up a batch of her favorite cookies. Then, everyone gathers at the appointed time at your home to taste each other's handiwork! It is best to send out the invitations about 2 weeks in advance so that your guests have time to choose their recipes. On the day of the exchange, have plenty of gallon-sized, zip-top bags on hand so that all the different cookies can be divided up among the guests and everyone ends up with a wonderful, assorted bag of homemade goodness to take back home and share with their families.

If you are in need of a few cookie recipes to inspire you, check out *Biggest Book of Cookies: 475 All-Time Favorites* from Better Homes & Gardens, or any of the other terrific cookie cookbooks out there.

A Recipe Swap

A recipe swap is exactly what it sounds like! Your friends are invited to your home to share their favorite recipes with everyone else. Have a stack of lined index cards in both the 3" x 5" size and the 4" x 6" size. (Those are the two common sizes that recipe card boxes come in.) It is also a nice idea to have markers and decorative-edged scissors on the table in case your guests would like to decorate the index cards after they copy out the recipes that they would like to add to their own collection. If you are keeping a homemaking notebook, you can also copy the recipes directly onto the note pages!

St. Meinrad, patron saint of hospitality, pray for us!

Spring

May Night

The spring is fresh and fearless
And every leaf is new,
The world is brimmed with moonlight,
The lilac brimmed with dew.

Here in the moving shadows
I catch my breath and sing—
My heart is fresh and fearless
And over-brimmed with spring.

—SARA TEASDALE

There was no trace of the fog now. The sky became bluer and bluer, and now there were white clouds hurrying across it from time to time. In the wide glades there were primroses. A light breeze sprang up which scattered drops of moisture from the swaying branches and carried cool, delicious scents against the faces of the travelers.

—The Lion, the Witch and the Wardrobe, *C.S. Lewis*

Spring! The very word calls to mind daffodils, Easter eggs and new life everywhere one looks. The days are warmer and picnics are once again possible, so grab a basket and a good friend or sibling and go out into the sunshine to celebrate a special feast or day.

There are many terrific feast days during the spring months, the greatest being Easter, the Resurrection of Our Lord. In March you might also have a friend or two over for an afternoon of drawing and sipping tea in honor of St. Catherine of Bologna, patroness of artists. Or in April, bake a lovely batch of scones to celebrate the feast of St. Zita, patroness of homemakers. Why not get together with friends for a seed exchange in honor of St. Isidore the Farmer, on the 15th of May? There are so many fun ways to show hospitality to friends and family during the spring. Listed on the next page are just a few ideas to get you started.

March, *the month honoring St. Joseph*:
St. Catherine of Bologna (9th)
St. Patrick (17th)
St. Joseph (20th)

April, *the month dedicated to the Blessed Sacrament*:
Easter
St. Bernadette of Lourdes (16th)
St. Zita (27th)
St. Catherine of Siena (29th)

May, *the month honoring the Blessed Virgin*:
St. Isidore the Farmer (15th)
St. Brendan the Navigator (16th)
St. Joan of Arc (30th)

Below are a few menu suggestions for your springtime teas and gatherings. Don't forget to read through a recipe completely before starting it!

Menu

Tea or Sparkling Raspberry Punch

Buttermilk Scones

Stuffed Eggs

Sugar Cookies

Sparkling Raspberry Punch
(Makes ten 8-ounce servings)

Ingredients:

20   ounces of frozen unsweetened raspberries

1¼   cups sugar

1   quart sparkling water (chilled)

The juice of 2 lemons

1   extra lemon sliced in thin rounds, for garnish (optional)

Directions:

1. Combine frozen raspberries and sugar in a large 3-quart saucepan. Cook over medium heat, stirring occasionally for 20–25 minutes, until all the sugar has dissolved.

2. With a potato masher, (or the bottom of a tall drinking glass) mash the raspberries thoroughly. Pour the mixture through a strainer, making sure to extract all the juice. Discard the pulp.

3. Squeeze the lemons and strain the juice. Add it to the raspberry juice.

4. Allow the raspberry juice to cool and then chill it in the refrigerator for four hours.

5. Pour the cold raspberry juice into a pitcher and slowly add the quart of chilled sparkling water. Do not pour too fast, as this will cause too much fizzing and foaming.

6. Carefully slice the extra lemon into rounds about ¼-inch thick. Make a small cut from the center of the slice out to one edge. Slip the cut onto the rim of the glass and pour in the cold punch. (You can serve it over ice, if desired.)

Buttermilk Scones
(Makes 8 scones)

These are the classic scones. Try them with one of the spreads on pages 103-105 for a scrumptious tea-time treat.

Ingredients:

2	cups all-purpose flour
⅓	cup sugar
1 ½	teaspoons baking powder
¼	teaspoon salt
½	teaspoon baking soda
6	tablespoons butter, chilled
½	cup buttermilk
1	large egg
1 ½	teaspoons vanilla extract

Directions:

1. Preheat oven to 400°.

2. Mix all of the *dry ingredients* together with mixing spoon in a large-sized mixing bowl.

3. Cut the butter into ½-inch cubes and mix them into the flour mixture with two knives (or your clean hands), until the mixture resembles coarse crumbs.

4. In a small bowl, stir together the buttermilk, egg and vanilla. Add the buttermilk mixture to the flour mixture and stir to combine. Gently knead the dough six to eight times. (If the dough seems too sticky, add another ⅛ cup of flour.) Be careful not to over knead or the scones will get too tough and not rise well.

5. Dust your clean hands with a little flour and pat the dough into an 8-inch circle on an ungreased baking sheet. Dust a serrated knife with flour and cut the dough into eight wedges. (Scones can also be gently shaped into rounds like biscuits.)

6. Bake for 20-25 minutes or until the top is lightly browned and a toothpick inserted into the center of a scone comes out clean, with no raw batter sticking to it.

7. Cool on the pan for 5 minutes, then transfer the scones to a wire cooling rack to cool. Re-cut into wedges, if necessary. Serve warm, or cool completely and store in an airtight container.

Basic Place Setting

This is an example of the traditional, basic place setting. The fork is on the left of the plate with the napkin, and the spoon with the knife (blade facing the plate) are placed on the right. For your own informal teas, it is perfectly acceptable to alter this arrangement by placing the napkin in the plate or any other creative variations.

Stuffed Eggs
(Makes 8 stuffed egg halves.)

Eggs are so plentiful (and inexpensive!) at this time of year. For a real treat, use real farm eggs. The yolks are such a bright yellow!

Ingredients:

4   large, hard-boiled eggs

3   tablespoons mayonnaise

⅛   teaspoon salt

     paprika (optional for garnish)

Directions:

1. To boil the eggs, place them in a small saucepan and cover them with cool water. Bring to a boil for 2 minutes, then turn off the heat and place the cover on the pan. After 20 minutes, run cold tap water over the eggs to cool them.

2. Peel the eggs and cut in half lengthwise with a knife. Carefully remove the yolks and place in a small bowl.

3. Add remaining ingredients (except the paprika) and blend together using a fork to mash the yolks while mixing well.

4. Carefully spoon the mixture back into the egg white halves, dividing the yolk mixture evenly between them. Garnish with a light sprinkling of paprika if desired and store in the refrigerator until ready to serve.

Tea & Cake

Sugar Cookies
(Makes 2 dozen cookies)

These simple cookies are wonderful topped with a bit of Easy Vanilla Icing (page 27) after they have cooled.

Ingredients:

1	cup butter, *softened*
1	cup sugar
1	egg
1	teaspoon vanilla extract
1	tablespoon milk
2½	cups flour
⅛	teaspoon salt
1	teaspoon baking powder

Directions:

1. Preheat oven to 375°.
2. Place *softened* butter in medium mixing bowl and add sugar. Mix butter and sugar together until creamy. You can use a hand mixer for this or a simple wooden spoon.
3. Stir in the egg, milk and vanilla.
4. Combine the flour, salt and baking powder in a separate bowl and mix until well blended.
5. Add the *dry ingredients* to the butter, egg and sugar mixture. Mix well to form a stiff dough.
6. Using clean hands, form dough into approximately 1–1½-inch balls (or roll out dough with a rolling pin and cut out shapes with cookie cutters) and place onto an ungreased *cookie sheet*, keeping cookies about 1½ inches apart. Gently flatten each cookie with your

hand or the bottom of a glass dipped in sugar.

7.　Bake for 8–9 minutes. Remove cookies from cookie sheet and cool on a wire rack.

These cookies also make terrific gifts! See below for a ready-made tag to attach to a small bag or box of cookies.

To:

From:

To:

From:

A Recipe Card

If you would like to share these (or any other) recipes with a friend, simply make copies of the recipe card provided below. Print them onto cardstock or any other stiff paper and cut out with plain or decorative-edged scissors. These make nice additions to your homemaking notebook, and it is also a thoughtful gesture to include the recipe when giving a gift of food.

A Recipe For: _____

Setting a Spring Table

When we think of spring, we think of color and flowers and all things light and lively. Try one or two (or more!) of the ideas below to give your tea table a fresh look for spring.

- Use a pretty floral sheet for a tablecloth.
- Use floral ladies handkerchiefs for delicate looking cloth napkins.
- Check flea markets for mismatched, floral-themed tea-cups and saucers. Use them all together for a table that looks like a bouquet!
- Save small glass bottles, such as those vanilla and other extracts come in, or salt shakers without their lids, to use for tiny vases. These are perfect for individual bouquets to set next to each person's plate.
- Tie a ribbon around a cloth napkin (not too tightly!) and tuck in a packet of easy-to-grow annuals like zinnias, morning glories or marigolds.

May Day Baskets

It is an old tradition for young people to leave "May baskets" hanging on the doorknobs of their friends and neighbors on the eve of May Day, the first of May. The May baskets would contain freshly picked flowers and perhaps a little note or message.

A very easy "May basket" can be made with recycled containers and decorated like the small, plastic yogurt cup to the left. Simply paint it a pretty color, glue on trim and attach a ribbon. The May basket can be filled with any available fresh flowers, candy or even a few sugar cookies tied up with ribbon in plastic wrap. Including a holy card depicting the Blessed Mother would also be a lovely touch!

Written in March

The cock is crowing,
The stream is flowing,
The small birds twitter,
The lake doth glitter
The green field sleeps in the sun;
The oldest and youngest
Are at work with the strongest;
The cattle are grazing,
Their heads never raising;
There are forty feeding like one!
Like an army defeated
The snow hath retreated,
And now doth fare ill
On the top of the bare hill;
The plowboy is whooping—anon-anon:
There's joy in the mountains;
There's life in the fountains;
Small clouds are sailing,
Blue sky prevailing;
The rain is over and gone!

—WILLIAM WORDSWORTH

A Garden for Mary

The tradition of a special garden devoted to Our Lady goes all the way back to medieval times, and possibly earlier. These beautiful gardens were filled with plants that were named for Our Lord and the Blessed Mother. They were little plots of earth, set aside and dedicated to honoring Mary by offering her those blooms, trees and berries which had been named for her.

Today, the traditional Mary garden is becoming popular once again! What a great way to honor Our Lady while at the same time growing lovely flowers and useful herbs to use while showing others hospitality. A small Mary garden can be tucked into a corner of an existing flower bed, or the corner of your back yard. If you live in an apartment or do not have room outdoors, you can make a container Mary garden in a large pot or window box. (Just make sure there are holes in the bottom for the excess water to drain out.) Most gardens, both large and small, which are dedicated to the Blessed Mother, have some sort of statue or plaque as the focal point of the garden. For a small container or window garden, a laminated picture would also work.

Prior to the time of Christ, many flowers, herbs, trees, etc. held the names of various pagan gods and goddesses. As Christianity spread, these plants were re-named for the

Blessed Mother, the saints and Our Lord. Over time, many of these names have been nearly forgotten. Below is a list of a few easy-to-grow flowers together with their traditional, Christian names. (For a more extensive list, see the further reading suggestions at the back of this book.)

- Morning Glory—Our Lady's Mantle
- Cornflower—Mary's Crown
- Pinks (Dianthus)—Mary's Pink
- Sweet Scabious—Mary's Pincushion
- Impatients—Mother Love
- Marigold—Mary's Gold
- Zinnia—The Virgin
- Petunia—Our Lady's Praises
- Daffodil—Mary's Star
- Sun Flower—Mary's Gold
- Sweet Pea—Mary's Foot
- Rose—Symbolizes Mary Herself
- Spearmint—Mary's Mint
- Thyme—A Symbol of the Virgin's Humility
- Rosemary—Mary's Nosegay
- Sage—Mary's Shawl
- Violet—Symbolizes Our Lady's Modesty

Planning Your Garden

Make sure, when choosing the location for your Mary garden, that the plants will receive at least 5 hours of sunlight each day. (Do not plant outdoors until the weather has warmed a little and there is no danger of a frost.) After you have decided on the spot for your garden, prepare the bed or container with lots of good, rich soil with a generous amount of compost mixed in. You will want the final dirt to be loose, not hard-packed, so that the roots can penetrate it easily.

When selecting your plants or seeds, look at the back of the seed packet, or the tag that comes with the plant, and make a note of what the mature height will be. (The height the plant will be when it is fully-grown.) You will want the tallest plants in the back of the flowerbed or container, and the shorter in the front. If you like, you can draw a simple sketch of your garden plan on paper. This will give you an idea of how the final Mary garden will look. Your garden sketch might look something like this:

Garden Plan

1...Zinnias
2...Marigolds
3...Petunias
4...Spearmint
5...Thyme
6...Stepping Stones

After you have planted your seeds or plants, sprinkle with water until the ground is thoroughly wet. Be very careful watering where tiny seeds have been planted, as it is very easy to wash them away before they sprout. Always use a watering can with a sprinkler nozzle so that the water falls like a gentle rain. Do not water too much, just enough each day to keep the soil damp, but not soggy. (Read the backs of the seed packets for specific growing information.) Once the plants are well established and the little seedlings are growing well, all that is required is to keep the soil moist and to pull any weeds that may come up. Picking off the spent blooms will also keep your Mary garden looking fresh and pretty. Be sure to make notes in the gardening section of your notebook about which plants grew better than others or which flowers and herbs you might like to try next year. Also include a few photos of your Mary garden so that you can remember its loveliness in the middle of winter.

The nicest thing about having your very own fresh flowers is being able to brighten another person's day with them. Collect little vases when you have the opportunity. Thrift stores and garage sales are excellent places to find many beautiful little vases for only a few cents each, and don't forget to re-use any small glass bottles from the kitchen that your mother does not need. It takes only a few blossoms to fill these little vases and make them look lovely. Do not forget to add a bit of greenery to your tiny arrangement with a sprig or two of herbs, some of which have very beautiful foliage! These petite bouquets are also the perfect little offerings to set next to the statues of Our Lady in your home.

St. Fiacre, patron saint of gardeners, pray for us!

A Seed Exchange & Apron

So many plants readily reproduce themselves, (such as mints and other herbs, day lilies, aloe vera, the ivies, etc.) and most packets of seeds contain more than is needed by one person with a small garden. By hosting a seed and plant exchange with other gardening friends, everyone shares in nature's bounty!

It might be a good idea to have this event out of doors, on a porch or perhaps a picnic table. If you save a few of the cardboard-type egg cartons and purchase a bag of potting soil, you and your guests can start some of the seeds in the little egg cups. (Be sure to write on the carton which types of seeds are planted where.) The nice thing about using the cardboard egg cartons for seedling pots is that when you are ready to move the little plants into your garden, you do not have to remove them from their paper pots. Simply cut the egg cups apart and plant the whole thing (cup and all) in the ground. The paper will soon disintegrate, allowing the roots to grow and spread.

Another fun project for a seed and plant exchange is for everyone to make their own gardening apron. (These also make lovely gifts for friends who like to garden!) Gardening aprons are much shorter than traditional aprons, to allow for much bending and kneeling on the ground. They also have large pockets for holding seeds, garden markers and tools, and they are usually made of a sturdy fabric.

To make an easy gardening apron, you will need:

- **Two placemats** (Be sure to read the tags on them before purchasing. They must say that the placemat is "machine washable.")

- **Between 1½ and 2 yards of 1-inch wide gros-grain ribbon** (For the exact length of ribbon, measure around your waist and add 1 yard (for the ties).

- **Thread to match**

Directions:

1. Wash and dry the placemats (following the directions on the fabric care tag) to pre-shrink them. Press flat and smooth, if necessary.

2. Fold the long side of one of the placemats over 1¼"
    and press. If your placemat has a right and wrong
    side, make sure to fold over to the wrong side. (See
    fig.1) This will form the casing for the ribbon ties.

FIG.1

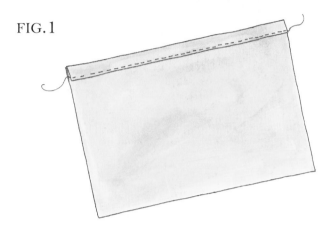

3. Take the second placemat, and measure down 7½"
    from one of the long edges and mark. Cut along this
    line. (See fig.2)

FIG.2

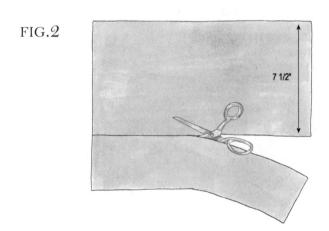

7 1/2"

4. Turn under (toward the wrong side) ½" along this cut
    edge and press.

5. Carefully pin the 7" section to the top of the first placemat, keeping the casing for the ribbon at the top and lining up all the edges. Make sure that the ½" turned up edge is even with the bottom of the first placemat. (See fig.3)

FIG.3

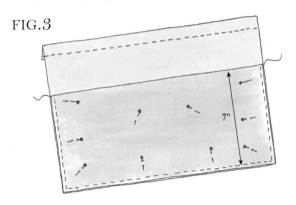

6. Stitch along the three sides of the lower 7" piece to form a pocket.

7. Next, measure in 5½" from each side of the apron pocket and mark. These 2 lines will divide the one large pocket into 3 smaller ones. Starting from the bottom, stitch along the markings (see fig.4) to form 3 pockets.

FIG.4

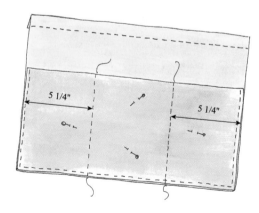

8. Now attach a large safety pin to the end of your ribbon, and thread it through the casing at the top of the apron. Center the ribbon in the apron and stitch across both ends of the casing to prevent the ribbon from being pulled out. (See fig.5)

FIG.5

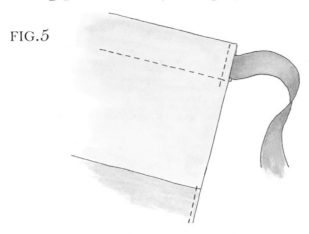

That's it! You now have a sturdy, useful gardening apron!

These little aprons also make *wonderful* craft aprons. The pockets make very handy places to stash supplies and tools while you are in the midst of a craft project.

Our Lady's Bug

Did you know that in Europe, during the Middle Ages, farmers would pray for Heaven's help in rescuing their crops from the plant-destroying aphids? Very often, these prayers were answered by the arrival of ladybugs, which came by the hundreds to devour the aphids. For this reason, the insect became know as "Our Lady's Bug," as the farmers believed that the Virgin Mary herself had sent them as an answer to their prayers.

Tea & Cake

Summer

A Summer Morning

I saw dawn creep across the sky,
And all the gulls go flying by.
I saw the sea put on its dress
Of blue midsummer loveliness,
And heard the trees begin to stir
Green arms of pine and juniper.
I heard the wind call out and say,
"Get up, my dear, it is today!"

—RACHEL FIELD

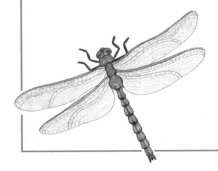

Even the sun, as it rose shining into the clearest of skies, seemed to know this day was the glorious Fourth. At breakfast Ma said, "This would be a perfect day for a Fourth of July picnic."

—LITTLE TOWN ON THE PRAIRIE, *LAURA INGALLS WILDER*

The hot summer sun is overhead, the days are longer and our pace has slowed down just a bit. It's the perfect season for leisurely lounging in the shade of a favorite tree with a friend, while sipping glasses of lemonade.

The summer months hold many beautiful feasts to celebrate. St. Anthony's (the patron saint of lost articles) feast day in June would be a great time to host a gathering where a scavenger hunt (or searching for "lost items") is the main event. In July, a fancy, old-fashioned tea would be a fun way to celebrate the feast of St. Maria Goretti, patroness of girls. And with all the lovely plants in bloom, the feasts of St. Fiacre or St. Rose of Lima (*both* patrons of gardeners and florists) would be wonderful occasions to bring a bouquet of flowers to a sick friend or perhaps a nursing home resident.

A Few Feasts to Celebrate

June, *the month honoring the Sacred Heart of Jesus:*
    St. Anthony of Padua (13th)
    St. Thomas More (22nd)
    Sts. Peter and Paul (29th)
July, *the month honoring the Precious Blood:*
    St. Elizabeth of Portugal (4th)
    St. Maria Goretti (6th)
    St. Benedict (11th)
August, *month dedicated to the Immaculate Heart of Mary:*
    St. Clare of Assisi (11th)
    St. Rose of Lima (23rd)
    St. Fiacre (30th)

Below are a few menu suggestions for your summertime teas and gatherings. Remember, the recipes below are only suggestions. Get creative!

Menu

Tea or Lemonade
Tea Biscuits

Cucumber Sandwiches
Vanilla Tea Cake

Lemonade

(Makes 2 quarts)

This is such a refreshing, old-fashioned–tasting lemonade!

Ingredients:

1   cup of lemon juice

1   cup sugar

1   lemon

Directions:

1. Combine lemon juice and sugar in 2-quart pitcher.

2. Fill the pitcher with water and stir until the sugar has dissolved.

3. Chill in refrigerator until ready to use. Before serving, slice the extra lemon into thin circles and float in pitcher.

4. Serve over ice. Enjoy!

Tea Biscuits

(Makes 1 dozen)

Ingredients:

2   cups all-purpose flour

4½   teaspoons baking powder

½   teaspoon salt

3   tablespoons butter

1   cup milk

Directions:

1.   Preheat oven to 450°.

2.   Mix all of the *dry ingredients* together with a wire whisk or mixing spoon in a medium-sized mixing bowl.

3.   Cut in butter or margarine, rubbing the butter into the dry ingredients with fingers.

4.   Make a shallow hole in the center of the dry ingredients with your fist. Add milk slowly to make a soft dough. The dough should be soft and pliable, but not sticky.

5.   Knead dough very lightly for a few seconds on a lightly floured surface. With lightly floured hands, shape the dough into slightly flattened balls about 3 inches across.

6.   Place biscuits on a greased cookie sheet and bake for 12–15 minutes or until lightly browned. Serve warm!

Liberty Teas

Tea was the most popular drink in America in 1773 when the men of Boston, sick and tired of the King of England's unfair tax, dumped 342 chests of black tea into the sea. The waves of patriotism set off by the Boston Tea Party caused nearly everyone in the thirteen colonies to turn their back on English tea. But what would they drink? The resourceful Americans soon turned to the herbs and flowers growing right in their own gardens and countryside. They began experimenting with various wild and domestic roots, leaves and berries and came up with many delicious combinations. The creative teas brewed during these Revolutionary War years were appropriately called the "Liberty Teas."

Cider cake is very good, to be baked in small loaves. One pound and a half of flour, half a pound of sugar, quarter pound of butter, half pint of cider, one teaspoonful of pearlash; spice to your taste. Bake till it turns easily in the pans. I should think about half an hour.

THE AMERICAN FRUGAL HOUSEWIFE, *LYDIA MARIE CHILD, 1833*

Cucumber Sandwiches

(Makes eight little tea sandwiches)

Prepare these classic tea sandwiches just before your guests arrive, so they are nice and fresh.

Ingredients:

1   3-ounce package cream cheese, softened (You can also use the whipped, flavored or plain cream cheese in the plastic tubs.)

4   slices of bread

1   cucumber

salt

Directions:

1.   Peel cucumber and cut into thin slices (¼" thick or less). Sprinkle with a little bit of salt and set aside.

2.   Carefully spread a thin layer of cream cheese on one side of each slice of bread.

3.   Arrange one layer of sliced cucumbers on two of the slices of bread. Cover with the remaining two slices. Using a serrated knife, carefully trim off the crusts and cut each sandwich into four quarters.

4.   Arrange on a pretty plate and enjoy!

Vanilla Tea Cake
(Serves 8)

Ingredients:

1½   cups all-purpose flour

1   cup sugar

1½   teaspoons baking powder

¼   teaspoon salt

⅔   cup milk

½   cup butter or margarine, *softened*

2   eggs

1   teaspoon vanilla

Powered sugar for dusting over finished cake

Directions:

1.   Preheat oven to 375°.

2.   In a large mixing bowl combine flour, sugar, baking powder and salt.

3. Add the milk, *softened* butter or margarine, egg and vanilla. Beat with an electric mixer on low speed until combined, then beat on medium speed for 1 minute. You can use a wire whisk if you do not have an electric mixer.

4. Pour the batter into a *greased and floured* (see side box at right for more information) 8-inch round or square baking pan.

5. Bake for 25 to 30 minutes or until a toothpick inserted in the center of the cake comes out without any raw batter sticking to it.

Greasing & Flouring

Using your hand or a paper towel spread an even layer of cooking oil over the bottom and sides of the cake pan.

Next, sprinkle a little flour in the bottom of the pan. Start with about a teaspoon and add more if necessary.

Tilt and tap the pan until the flour covers all the surfaces. Now tap out any excess flour. Your pan is now ready for the cake batter to be poured in.

6. Let the cake cool for 15 minutes in the pan. Then remove from the pan and let cool completely on a wire cooling rack.

7. When the cake is completely cool, set it on a plate and dust with powdered sugar. Delicious!

A Recipe Card

If you would like to share these (or any other) recipes with a friend, simply make copies of the recipe card provided below. Print them onto cardstock or any other stiff paper and cut out with plain or decorative-edged scissors. These make nice additions to your homemaking notebook, and it is also a thoughtful gesture to include the recipe when giving a gift of food.

A Recipe For:

A Few Ideas for Summer Teas

- Dropping a few fresh raspberries or a fresh strawberry into your teacup before pouring in the hot tea is a fun way to freshen up a summer cup of tea.

- When the outside temperatures begin to climb, don't forget about iced tea!

- For interesting ice cubes, try placing clean mint leaves in the water in an ice-cube tray, and freezing. These mint-cubes also go very well with lemon-ade.

- For a simple, summery napkin ring, wrap the stem of an artificial flower (one with a wire in the stem) in a small circle and insert the napkin.

- Do not underestimate the beauty of a few wildflowers in a simple jar on your tea table.

- Remember, we all have daily opportunities to practice hospitality, kindness and service with family as well as friends.

Spiritual Bouquet Cards

The sweet tradition of sending a loved one a little note or card, which lists specific prayers being prayed for them, has been around for many years. It is called a "spiritual bouquet" because your prayers and devotions are gathered together like a lovely bouquet and offered up to God on behalf of the person you give the card to. Spiritual bouquet cards are great to give along with another gift or all by themselves. What a beautiful thing it would be to slip one under the pillow of a sleeping sibling or tuck one in your father's coat pocket!

To get started right away, make copies (on plain or decorative paper) of the spiritual bouquet card provided on the next page and place a number on the blank preceding the prayer to indicate how many you will be offering. Or, design your own card with any prayers or devotions you like, as it makes the gift that much more personal!

A Gift of Prayer

I Will Offer for You & Your Intentions:

____ Our Fathers

____ Hail Mary's

____ Rosaries

____ Holy Communions

____ Holy Hours

____ Masses

A Gift of Prayer

August

Deep in the wood I made a house
Where no one knew the way;
I carpeted the floor with moss,
And there I loved to play.

I heard the bubbling of the brook;
At times an acorn fell,
And far away a robin sang
Deep in the lonely dell.

I set a rock with acorn cups;
So quietly I played
A rabbit hopped across the moss,
And did not seem afraid.

That night before I went to bed
I at my window stood,
And thought how dark my house must be
Down in the lonesome wood.

—KATHARINE PYLE

Picnicking

*At last the sun was overhead, and Pa stopped the horses
by a little creek. It was good to feel still. The little creek
talked to itself, the horses munched their oats in the feed-
box at the back of the wagon, and on the warm grass
Ma spread a cloth and opened the lunch box. There was
bread and butter and good hardboiled eggs, with pepper
and salt in a paper, to dip the bitten eggs into.*

—By the Shores of Silver Lake, *Laura Ingalls Wilder*

What could be more enjoy-
able on a summer afternoon
than a picnic! Picnics are
perfect for so many occa-
sions and can be kept quite
simple and spontaneous.
Travel to a nearby park or
only as far as a shady spot
in your own backyard. If you
keep your picnic basket supplied with all
the necessities but food, it will be a simple task to invite a
friend to a picnic at a moment's notice. If you do not have
a traditional picnic basket, what about a small plastic laun-
dry basket, plastic storage crate or even a dish tub? These
all come in a rainbow of colors and are quite sturdy. Fill
them with a few supplies and top with a colorful and coordinating cloth (an old quilt, blanket or tablecloth) and you
have a very pretty picnic kit ready to go!

Tea & Cake

Below are a few ideas of what to include in your picnic kit:

- A little first-aid kit with a small bottle of sunscreen, a few band-aids and antibacterial ointment.

- Stitch a small (about 4" x 6") drawstring bag and stuff a few empty, plastic grocery sacks inside to hold the trash.

- Put in a few paper or plastic plates and cups and a few napkins.

- Make self-chilling water bottles by filling plastic water bottles (re-use water and juice bottles) or mason jars ⅓ full with water and putting them in the freezer the night before your picnic. Before packing them in your basket, fill them the rest of the way up with water. As the ice melts, your water will stay nice and cold!

- A damp wash cloth, folded and placed inside a zip-top bag, is great to have on hand for any sticky cleanups.

- A small jar (½ pint or even a cleaned-out baby food jar) with a tight-fitting lid filled with water is the perfect thing to place those fresh-picked wildflowers in!

- A thermos for keeping hot tea hot and cold lemonade cold.

Do not stress about picnic food! If you keep the fare simple and easy to prepare, you will be more likely to actually go. For years the British people have enjoyed a simple, traditional, picnic-friendly meal that they call a "ploughman's lunch." It consists of a thick slice of cheese, a nice piece of crusty bread with butter, and a pickle. Frequently, some sort of fruit, such as an apple, and a hard-boiled egg are added to the meal.

If this is not to your liking, simply make a few of your favorite sandwiches, and on a hot day, bring along some cold lemonade in a thermos or even a quart jar. When making your sandwiches, try using pita bread (a flat, pocket bread) instead of regular sliced bread as it does not get squished as easily in a full picnic basket.

Picnics are not just for the spring and summer months. Autumn is a wonderful time for outdoor hospitality! The sun is not as hot (there is no need to hunt for shade), and there are not nearly as many bugs! For a simple, warming snack, wrap a few fresh-out-of-the-oven muffins in a clean dish towel, and fill your thermos with piping hot tea or chocolate. If you would prefer a heartier meal, fill the thermos with hot soup (in addition to the muffins) and pack a mug and spoon for yourself and your guest.

After a successful picnic, make a note of what you liked about it in a special picnic section of your homemaking

Tea & Cake

notebook. Include the foods you served, the time of year and the location. This information will make it even easier to go on future picnics. So pack up your picnic basket (or box, or crate) and grab a friend, sibling, or even a parent! Enjoy a bit of the great outdoors while showing hospitality to someone special.

The Rat brought the boat alongside the bank, made her fast, helped the still awkward Mole safely ashore, and swung out the luncheon-basket. The Mole begged as a favour to be allowed to un-pack it all by himself; and the Rat was very pleased to let him, and to sprawl at full length on the grass and rest, while his excited friend shook out the tablecloth and spread it, took out all the mysterious packets one by one and arranged their contents in due order still gasping, "O my! O my!" at each fresh revelation.

—The Wind in the Willows, Kenneth Grahame

The Gift of a Letter

How frequently do we hear persons exclaiming, that they do not know what to write about! Such an observation is a disgrace to the person who makes it. Were the mother, the sister, the cousin, friend, or even acquaintance, to enter the room in which you are sitting...would you have nothing to say?

—Young Lady's Own Book, *1836*

In days past, before the telephone and long before email, letters were the way that people communicated with each other. Most of these letters were handwritten and became treasured gifts to the recipient. Why not revive the tradition among your friends and relatives? There is something so special about holding a hand written letter in your hands and being able to curl up in a cozy spot to read and re-read it.

Did you know that the pre-made envelope did not come into widespread use until the 1830's? Before this time, it was standard practice to simply use a standard sheet of paper folded in such a way as to enclose your folded letter. In another section, the *Young Lady's Own Book* says, "A single sheet of paper is sufficient for a note and its envelope." It goes on to explain how to fold the sheet of paper in half (so that you have a 5½" x 8½" rectangle) and write only on the front and back of one half of the paper leaving one side blank. The letter is then folded (see picture on opposite page) so that the blank side is facing out so that it can be addressed in the usual manner.

You can also make your own envelopes out of beautiful papers such as wrapping paper, scrapbooking papers or even wall paper! To get the right shape, gently open up a regular envelope all the way, and trace around this pattern. (If the scrapbook or wrapping paper is too thin, glue another sheet of regular paper, in a coordinating color, to the backside of the wrapping paper first to help stiffen it. The second sheet will be inside your envelope like a liner.)

To form the envelope, simply fold it as your pattern was folded and glue in the appropriate places. When it comes to addressing your envelope, don't worry about the beautiful prints: simply write the address on a little label cut from regular white paper and trimmed with decorative-edged scissors, or purchase pre-made, plain white label stickers. After the glue has dried completely, you can gently press the final envelope with a slightly warm iron to make it smooth and crisp. To seal your envelope you can use a few drops of glue under the flap, tape or a pretty sticker.

On special occasions, it is also a fun idea to enclose a small gift in your correspondence. (Be sure to weigh your letter so that you include the proper postage.) A few ideas are a favorite recipe on a pretty card, seed packets, a spiritual bouquet card (see pages 73-74), tea bags or even a pretty book marker. You might like to tie up the letters that you receive with a piece of ribbon, or sew a small drawstring bag to store them in. It does not have to be perfect: just write a letter and brighten someone's day! A letter is a gift of yourself, a gift of your time.

St. Francis de Sales, patron saint of writers, pray for us!

Various are the occasions on which ladies are called upon to exercise their skill in the art of epistolary composition: this, generally speaking, is the only style of writing of which they will find it inconvenient to be ignorant.

—Young Lady's Own Book, *1836*

Autumn

Autumn

The morns are meeker than they were,
The nuts are getting brown;
The berry's cheek is plumper,
The rose is out of town.

The maple wears a gayer scarf,
The field a scarlet gown.
Lest I should be old-fashioned,
I'll put a trinket on.

—EMILY DICKINSON

The sun was low, and the heavens glowed with the splendor of an autumn sunset. Gold and purple clouds lay on the hilltops, and rising high into the ruddy light were silvery white peaks that shone like the airy spires of some Celestial City.

—LITTLE WOMEN, *LOUISA MAY ALCOTT*

Ah, the summer heat has subsided. There is a delightful nip in the air, and the green leaves are beginning to blush to shades of crimson and gold. The comforting aromas of baking bread and spiced hot cider seem to belong to this season, together with the crackle of dried leaves and wood fires.

There are so many wonderful saints whose feast days occur within the autumn months. You could have a special party for Our Lady on her birthday, September 8th. In October, why not have a tea honoring our Guardian Angels, who do so very much for us? Or, if you play an instrument, November 22nd (the feast of St. Cecilia, the patroness of music, musicians and poetry) is a wonderful occasion to invite a musical friend over for tea and music making. The brief list on the next page may be used as a starting point for ideas for celebrating during this lovely season.

A Few Feasts to Celebrate

September, *the month dedicated to Our Lady of Sorrows:*
   Feast of the Nativity of the Blessed Virgin Mary (8th)
   St. Nicholas of Tolentino (10th)
   Feast of the Archangels (29th)
October, *the month dedicated to the most Holy Rosary:*
   St. Therese (1st)
   The Guardian Angels (2nd)
   St. Francis of Assisi (4th)
November, *the month dedicated to the Holy Souls in Purgatory:*
   All Saints Day (1st)
   St. Elizabeth of Hungary (17th)
   St. Cecilia (22nd)

The following menu suggestions would work equally well for the above feasts, name days, or just about any occasion you can dream up!

Menu

Tea or Hot Cider

Parmesan Herb Bread

Smoked Ham Sandwiches

Molasses Cookies

Hot Spiced Cider

(Makes eight 8-ounce servings)

This recipe can be divided in half, but it keeps well in the refrigerator and can be stored in the original cider bottle.

Ingredients:

1   64-ounce bottle apple cider
2   cinnamon sticks
1   teaspoon whole allspice
1   teaspoon whole cloves

Directions:

1.   In a 3-quart saucepan (or larger), combine apple cider, cinnamon sticks (broken once or twice), allspice and cloves. If you would rather not have the spices floating loose in the cider, wrap them in a small piece of cheesecloth or loosely woven, pre-washed muslin.

2.   Bring to a boil over high heat. Reduce heat, and keep warm.

Parmesan Herb Bread

(Makes 1 loaf)

Remember, when mixing *quickbreads,* be careful
not to over mix. Stir just until blended.

Ingredients:

2	cups all-purpose flour
3	teaspoons baking powder
1	teaspoon salt
2	teaspoons Italian seasoning
½	teaspoon onion powder
½	teaspoon garlic powder
½	teaspoon dried parsley
¼	cup Parmesan cheese
¼	cup melted butter or margarine
1	cup milk

Directions:

1. Preheat oven to 400°.

2. Mix all of the *dry ingredients* together with a wire whisk or mixing spoon in a medium-sized mixing bowl. In a separate bowl, combine the *wet ingredients* and mix thoroughly with the whisk or spoon.

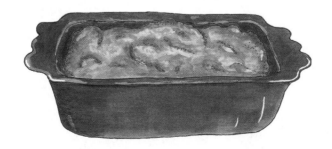

3. Now carefully pour the wet ingredients into the bowl containing the dry ingredients and mix just until combined. A few lumps are ok; do not over mix!

4. Pour the stiff batter into a greased loaf pan (9" x 5" or a similar size) and bake for 40 to 45 minutes, or until an inserted toothpick comes out clean.

5. Allow bread to cool 10 minutes in the pan, then remove from pan to finish cooling.

A Gift Idea

This *quickbread* recipe also makes a lovely gift. You can give it freshly baked and still warm from the oven, or as a mix. To make the "mix," simply stir all of the dry ingredients together and pour them into a quart-sized, zip-top plastic bag. Package the plastic bag in a simple, brown paper lunch bag with the top folded over and a pretty ribbon laced through two holes punched through the bag top. Attach a copy of the gift tag on page 97 or make your own. What a welcome gift!

The meat was laid on a board in the back-door shed, and every piece was sprinkled with salt. The hams and the shoulders were put to pickle in brine, for they would be smoked, like the venison, in the hollow log. "You can't beat hickory-cured ham," Pa said.

—LITTLE HOUSE IN THE BIG WOODS, *LAURA INGALLS WILDER*

Smoked Ham Sandwiches with Honey Mustard

(Makes four whole sandwiches or eight small ones.)

Today we have only to make a trip to the deli of our local grocery store to find smoked ham, but I'm sure Pa's was delicious! Here is a recipe for a lovely honey mustard that goes very well with smoked ham.

Ingredients for Honey Mustard:

¼   cup Dijon-style mustard
2   tablespoons honey

Directions:

1. In a small bowl, combine the mustard and honey until well blended.

2. Store in the refrigerator in an airtight container until you are ready to use it. Makes enough for four sandwiches.

Ingredients for the Ham Sandwiches:

8   slices of bread or rolls, etc.

8   slices of smoked ham cut medium to thin

Directions:

1. Choose your favorite bread. This can be anything from simple sliced bread to small rolls. If using rolls or any other unsliced bread, carefully slice lengthwise with a serrated knife.

2. Spread the honey mustard onto one side of each the slices or rolls. Arrange two slices of ham per sandwich. You may have to adjust the amount of ham or trim and fold it to fit the bread you are using.

3. If you are using ordinary slices of bread, carefully trim off the crusts and cut each sandwich in half diagonally twice so that you have four small triangles per sandwich. Arrange on a pretty plate.

It is best to make sandwiches just before they are to be eaten. If you should need to make them ahead of time, cover the plate with plastic wrap so they do not dry out and store in the refrigerator.

Molasses and Ginger Cookies
(Makes 2 dozen cookies)

These cookies are full of delicious, autumn-smelling spices! Make a batch for a tea or as a wonderful gift.

Ingredients:

2¼   cups all-purpose flour
1   teaspoon baking soda
2   teaspoons ground ginger
1   teaspoon cinnamon
½   teaspoon ground cloves
¼   teaspoon salt
1   cup sugar
¾   cup butter, *softened*
1   egg
¼   cup molasses
¼   cup extra sugar for rolling cookies in

Directions:

1.   Preheat oven to 350°.

2.   Place *softened* butter in medium mixing bowl and add sugar. Mix butter and sugar together until creamy. You can use a hand mixer for this or a simple wooden spoon.

3.   Stir in the egg.

4.   Combine the rest of the *dry ingredients* in a separate bowl and mix with a wire whisk until well blended.

5.   Add the dry ingredients to the butter, egg and sugar mixture. Mix well to form a stiff dough.

6. Using clean hands, form dough into approximately 1–1½ inch balls and roll in sugar placed in a small bowl. Place sugared balls onto an ungreased *baking sheet*, keeping cookies about 1½ inches apart.

7. Bake for 12–15 minutes. Remove from cookie sheet and cool on a wire rack.

Who Was Fannie Farmer?

Fannie Farmer was born in 1857. She was the director of the Boston Cooking School from 1891 until 1902, when she decided to start "Miss Farmer's School of Cookery." Her greatest contribution was *The Boston Cooking-School Cook Book*, which she published in 1896. This cookbook was the first of its kind in that it gave specific and accurate measurements for the ingredients. Until this time, recipes were vague and not very dependable. Her cookbook made it possible for everyone to learn to cook with delicious results each and every time!

A Recipe Card

If you would like to share these (or any other) recipes
with a friend, simply make copies of the recipe card provided below. Print them onto cardstock or any other stiff
paper and cut out with plain or decorative-edged scissors.
These make nice additions to your homemaking notebook.
and it is also a thoughtful gesture to include the recipe
when giving a gift of food.

A Recipe For:

Decorating Ideas

One way to add a touch of autumn to your tea table is to simply go outside and bring a bit of nature in! For a quick and lovely centerpiece, simply tuck a few, well-chosen fall leaves around the base of a small pumpkin or even a large pinecone. For a more elaborate version, to use for a special family dinner perhaps, begin with some sort of shallow container 8–10 inches in diameter. A shallow bowl or basket or even a plate or pie dish will work. Now, carefully arrange an assortment of small pumpkins, gourds, fruit or pinecones in the container. Next, tuck in a few leaves and twigs gathered from outside. Finally, sprinkle the entire arrangement with a few, well-placed nuts.

A simple place card can be made by painting your friend's name onto a colorful fall leaf. Collect a few pretty leaves and press them between two sheets of waxed paper with a medium-hot iron for 10 seconds. After they have cooled completely, use a white paint pen (or a small paint brush and acrylic paints) to write in the names. Tie a bit of ribbon or jute string around a cloth napkin, tuck the leaf into the bow, and lay the napkin in the plate. That's it!

Another Gift Idea

For a quick and easy fall gift for your guests or a gracious hostess, tie up a few extra bundles of the mulling spices used in the spiced cider recipe and attach a tag explaining how to use them. Simply cut out several 6-inch squares of pre-washed and dried muslin and lay them out on a flat surface. Make a little pile of the spices in the center of each muslin square. Pull up the edges of the fabric to form a little pouch and secure with a rubber band. To finish off, tie a pretty ribbon over the rubber band and attach a copy of the tag on the next page or make your own!

If you are using the bundles as favors for your guests, you can place them in a pretty bowl or dish near the door so that they may take one as they leave. If you are using them as a *hostess gift*, it would be nice to tie three of the mulling spice bundles together with the same ribbon and attach a single tag.

Mulling Spices

...for making delicious spiced apple cider!

To make hot, spiced apple cider, pour 2 quarts
(64 oz.) of apple cider into a 3 quart saucepan.
Remove the ribbon and tag and drop this little
bag into the pot. Bring the cider to a boil over
high heat, stirring occasionally, then reduce heat
to low to keep warm. Enjoy!!

Parmesan Herb Bread Mix

Makes 1 loaf

* 1 Package Parmesan Herb Bread Mix
* 1 Cup of Milk
* 1/4 Cup Melted Butter

Preheat oven to 375. In a large mixing bowl,
combine the bread mix with the beer, beating
the mixture with a wooden spoon. The batter
will be lumpy. Place the batter in a greased loaf
pan. Pour the melted butter over the dough.
Bake for 50 - 55 minutes, or until golden.
Remove the bread from the oven. Allow to cool
slightly, slice and serve warm. Enjoy!!!

Autumn Fires

In the other gardens
And all up the vale,
From the autumn bonfires
See the smoke trail!

Pleasant summer over
And all the summer flowers,
The red fire blazes,
The grey smoke towers.

Sing a song of seasons!
Something bright in all!
Flowers in the summer,
Fires in the fall!

—ROBERT LOUIS STEVENSON

Beautify Your Bedroom

Now I'm going to imagine things into this room so that they'll always stay imagined. The floor is covered with a white velvet carpet with pink roses all over it and there are pink silk curtains at the windows. The walls are hung with gold and silver brocade tapestry. The furniture is mahogany. I never saw any mahogany, but it does sound so luxurious.

—ANNE OF GREEN GABLES, *L.M. MONTGOMERY*

Your bedroom is a place for you (or you and your siblings) to relax, read, write and pray. You may not dream of white velvet carpet and mahogany furniture, but it should be a peaceful area where you are happy to have your friends come when they are over for a visit. It need not be perfectly decorated or spotlessly clean for hospitality, but everyone will be more comfortable and have a better time if it is neat and organized. But what if your room is not as tidy and clean as you would like it? Listed below are a few tips to help you (and anyone else who shares the room) get rid of the clutter and make it a lovely place to be.

- The first thing to do, before attempting to clean, is to get rid of the extra stuff cluttering up your room. The easiest way to do this is to get three boxes and label them "throw away," "give away" and "put away". The "throw away" box is for anything that is broken beyond repair or is trash. The "give away" box is for things that are still useful, but that you do not need any longer. This box can be taken to Goodwill or any other charity when you are finished de-cluttering. The "put away" box is for items that belong in other areas of the house. You can take this box and put its contents away when you are done working for the day.

- Begin by choosing an area of your room to start with, such as under the bed. Pull out things, one at a time, and either put them where they belong in your room, or place them in one of the three boxes. Work only for 20 to 30 minutes at a time, getting a little more done each day. If you work too long at one time, you will get burnt out and not want to continue the job the next day.

- After cleaning out under the bed and leaving only those things which belong there (such as plastic boxes containing organized things), go on to the next area of your room that needs work. Maybe the closet or the top of your chest of drawers or a chair in your room. Go through each area with the three boxes until your entire room is free of clutter.

Now that your room has been freed of its excess stuff, you will need to organize the things that you have decided to keep. First, decide which items can be grouped together (such as letters, hair accessories, craft projects, etc.), and then think about what types of containers these items could be stored in. Clear plastic boxes are inexpensive and come in many convenient sizes. (You can even label them with a permanent marker.) If you want to hide the contents of your storage containers, try using baskets with lids. For smaller items, colorful cardboard photo boxes are a pretty alternative. Most of these even come with little label holders on one end so that you can see what is in each box at a glance. A quick look around your home will probably produce even more containers that can be used for organizing your things.

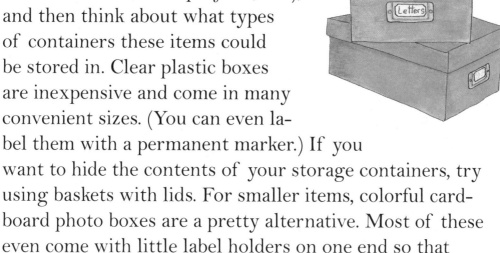

For photos and other paper items, consider hanging a cork board on one of your walls. The plain wooden frames of these boards can be easily decorated with paint or by gluing on small items such as buttons or silk flowers. A hanging, fabric shoe organizer works well for shoes, but also for many other small items such as little stuffed animals or dolls. Some of these are made to hang on the back of your bedroom door, while others are designed to hang from your closet pole.

Basic Maintenance

To maintain an organized room, spend 5 minutes at the end of each day putting any items back in their place. If you try to cultivate the habit of putting things back where they belong when you are finished using them, this task will take *less* than 5 minutes!

A simple weekly light cleaning routine is all that is needed to keep your room beautiful. (If you would like, write in your cleaning schedule on a page in your homemaking notebook.) Start by emptying the trash can and putting away any stray items. Next, slightly dampen a cloth napkin with water and dust the surfaces of the room. Surfaces could include the top of your chest of drawers, shelves, chairs, etc. Just look around and wipe wherever you see dust. After dusting, sweep or vacuum the floor and you are done!

St. Martha, patroness of homemakers, pray for us!

> *For God is not a God of disorder but of peace.*
>
> 1 CORINTHIANS 14:33

Delicious Spreads

Even though muffins and scones are quite good on their own, there is nothing quite like adding a touch of creamy honey butter or sweet vanilla cream cheese to accompany your quickbreads and tea biscuits. Yum!

Vanilla Cream Cheese
(Makes about ⅓ cup)

Ingredients:

1   3-ounce package cream cheese, *softened*
1   teaspoon vanilla
2   tablespoons powdered sugar

Directions:

1.   Stir ingredients well to combine.

2.   Transfer to a small serving crock or teacup. (Wonderful on warm scones!)

Strawberry Butter
(Makes about ½ cup)

½   cup butter, *softened*
⅓   cup powdered sugar
1   tablespoon strawberry preserves

Directions:

1. Combine all ingredients in a small bowl.

2. Beat at medium speed until creamy, scraping bowl often. Cover; refrigerate until serving time.

3. Transfer to a small serving bowl or dish.

Honey Butter
(Makes about ¼ cup)

¼ cup butter (½ of a stick), *softened*

1 tablespoon honey (Or use maple syrup for a scrumptious Maple Butter!)

Directions:

1. Stir ingredients well to combine.

2. Transfer to a small serving crock or teacup. (Delicious on muffins!)

Herbed Cream Cheese Spread
(Makes 1 cup)

1   8-ounce package cream cheese, *softened*

1   teaspoon Italian seasoning

½   teaspoon garlic powder

½   teaspoon onion powder

Directions:

1.   Stir ingredients well to combine.

2.   Allow the flavors to blend by storing in an air-tight container in the refrigerator for at least one hour.

3.   Transfer to a small serving bowl.

For more tea party ideas and recipes:

> *Totally Teatime Cookbook* by Helene Siegel and Karen Gillingham
> *Let's Have a Tea Party* by Emilie Barnes
> *The Anne of Green Gables Cookbook* by Kate Macdonald
> *The Louisa May Alcott Cookbook* by Gretchen Anderson
> *The Fannie Farmer Junior Cookbook* by Joan Scobey

If you would like to learn more about Mary Gardens:

> *Mary's Flowers: Gardens, Legends, and Meditations* by Vincenzina Krymow
> *Catholic Traditions in the Garden* by Ann Ball.
> Visit the gardening section of your local library for a wealth of information for the beginning gardener.

To learn more about Fannie Farmer:

> *Fannie in the Kitchen* by Deborah Hopkinson

Glossary of Terms

Cookie Sheet

A flat, rectangular pan with low, or no sides used for baking cookies.

Dry Ingredients

The ingredients in a recipe which are not wet or damp. Examples include flour, sugar, baking powder, spices and salt.

Greased (and Floured)

Pans are greased and floured to prevent the cakes or sweet breads from sticking. For a complete description of greasing and flouring, see page 26.

Hostess Gift

A small gift given to your hostess, when going to someone's home for a visit.

Mulling Spices

A mix of various spices meant for steeping in a warm beverage such as apple cider or in plain water to scent a room.

Name Days

The feast day of the Saint who shares your name.

Quickbread

Any breads (including muffins, biscuits and pancakes) using baking powder or baking soda for leavening instead of yeast. Yeast requires a long rising time to produce a fluffy bread, while baking soda and baking powder allow you to bake the bread right away.

Soften

To soften cream cheese or butter, simply take them out of the refrigerator about 30 minutes to an hour before you will need them for a recipe. Set them on the counter or table near your work area and they will be nice and soft when you need them.

Toothpick Test	A test used to determine whether or not baked items are done cooking. To perform a toothpick test, simply insert a clean, dry toothpick into the center of the baked item and pull it out. If it comes out with uncooked batter on it, you know that the item needs to be cooked slightly longer. If the toothpick comes out clean, the baked goods are done cooking.
Wet Ingredients	The ingredients in a recipe which are wet or damp. Examples include water, eggs, milk and vanilla extract.